the little book of
pink cocktails

An Hachette UK Company
www.hachette.co.uk

First published in Great Britain in 2024
by Hamlyn, an imprint of
Octopus Publishing Group Ltd
Carmelite House, 50 Victoria
Embankment, London EC4Y 0DZ
www.octopusbooks.co.uk

Distributed in the US by
Hachette Book Group
1290 Avenue of the Americas
4th and 5th Floors,
New York, NY 10104

Distributed in Canada by
Canadian Manda Group
664 Annette St.
Toronto, Ontario, Canada M6S 2C8

ISBN 978-0-7537-3555-8

A CIP catalogue record for this book is
available from the British Library

Printed and bound in China

10 9 8 7 6 5 4 3 2 1

Publisher: Lucy Pessell
Designer: Isobel Platt
Editor: Feyi Oyesanya
Assistant Editor: Samina Rahman
Production Manager: Lucy Carter
and Nic Jones

The measure that has been used in
the recipes is based on a bar jigger,
which is 25 ml (1 fl oz). If preferred, a
different volume can be used, providing
the proportions are kept constant within
a drink and suitable adjustments are
made to spoon measurements, where
they occur.

Standard level spoon measurements are
used in all recipes.

1 tablespoon = one 15 ml spoon
1 teaspoon = one 5 ml spoon

This book contains cocktails made with
raw or lightly cooked eggs. It is prudent
for more vulnerable people to avoid
uncooked or lightly cooked cocktails
made with eggs.

MIX
Paper | Supporting
responsible forestry
FSC
www.fsc.org   FSC® C144853

This FSC® label means that materials
used for the product have been
responsibly sourced

the little book of
pink
cocktails

50 pink cocktails, spritzes & punches

hamlyn

introduction

Let's celebrate these pretty-in-pink cocktails!

Creating the perfect pink cocktail involves balancing sweet and tart flavours, and the colour is both refreshing and enticing. You can choose from classics like the Strawberry Daiquiri to new creations like the Blackwood Blush. These rosy cocktails are sure to delight your taste buds whether you're hosting a party or just enjoying a lazy afternoon. So grab your shaker and be prepared to impress your guests with these fabulous pink elixirs.

contents

fizzes, highballs & collinses

fresh paloma

½ pink grapefruit, peeled

2 measures blanco tequila

2 measures soda water

1 teaspoon agave syrup

To decorate

pink grapefruit wedge

thyme

Juice the pink grapefruit and add the juice to a glass full of ice.

Add the remaining ingredients to the glass, garnish and serve.

flora dora

½ teaspoon sugar syrup

juice of ½ lime

½ teaspoon grenadine

2 measures gin

dry ginger ale, to top

lime twist, to decorate

Add ice, sugar syrup, lime juice, grenadine and gin into a cocktail shaker, and shake until a frost forms.

Pour without straining into a tall glass.

Top with dry ginger ale, garnish and serve.

watermelon spritz

4 chunks watermelon, plus slice, to decorate

2 measures lemon vodka

2 measures bitter lemon

1 measure apple juice

4 teaspoons lemon juice

3 teaspoons agave syrup

1 sprig mint

2 measures soda water, to top

Add the watermelon to a cocktail shaker and muddle.

Add the vodka, apple juice, mint, lemon juice and the agave syrup.

Shake and strain into a sling glass full of ice and top with soda water.

Garnish and serve.

sea breeze

1 measure vodka

2 measures cranberry juice

1 measure grapefruit juice

lime wedges to decorate

Fill a highball glass with ice, pour over the vodka, cranberry juice and grapefruit juice and stir well.

Garnish and serve.

berry collins

✦

4 raspberries, plus extra to decorate

1–2 dashes strawberry syrup

2 measures gin

2 teaspoons lemon juice sugar syrup, to taste

soda water, to top

To decorate

lemon slice

mint sprig

Muddle the raspberries and strawberry syrup in the bottom of each glass, then fill each glass with crushed ice.

Add the gin, lemon juice and sugar syrup.

Stir, then top with soda water.

Garnish and serve.

bay breeze

1 measure vodka

2 measures cranberry juice

1 measure pineapple juice

lime wedge, to decorate

Fill a highball glass with ice, pour over the vodka, cranberry juice and pineapple juice and stir well.

Garnish and serve.

singapore sling

1 measure gin
½ measure cherry brandy
¼ measure Cointreau
¼ measure Bénédictine
½ measure grenadine
½ measure lime juice
5 measures pineapple juice
1 dash Angostura bitters

To decorate
pineapple wedges
maraschino cherries

Half-fill a cocktail shaker with ice and put some more ice into a highball glass.

Add the remaining ingredients to the shaker and shake until a frost forms on the outside of the shaker.

Strain over the ice into the glass.

Garnish and serve.

pink cooler

5 chunks watermelon, plus extra, to decorate	Add the watermelon to a cocktail shaker and muddle.
2 measures lemon vodka	Add the vodka and shake.
2 measures bitter lemon	Strain into a glass full of ice and top with the bitter lemon.
	Garnish and serve.

gin sling

3 measures gin

1 measure cherry brandy

juice of ½ lemon

soda water, to top

Half-fill a cocktail shaker with ice and add some more ice into a highball glass.

Add the gin, cherry brandy and lemon to the shaker and shake until a frost forms on the outside of the shaker.

Strain over the ice into the glass, top with soda water and serve.

playa del mar

1 orange slice

light brown sugar and sea salt, mixed

1 ¼ measures tequila gold

1 ¼ measures Grand Marnier

2 teaspoons lime juice

1 measure cranberry juice

1 measure pineapple juice

To decorate

pineapple wedges

orange rind spirals

Frost the rim of the glass by moistening it with an orange slice, then pressing it into the sugar and salt mixture, and fill the glass with ice.

Pour the tequila, Grand Marnier and fruit juices into a cocktail shaker.

Fill the shaker with ice and shake vigorously for 10 seconds, and strain into the glass.

Garnish and serve.

bitter spring

1 measure Aperol

2 measures
grapefruit juice

4 measures soda water

grapefruit wedge,
to decorate

Add the Aperol, grapefruit juice
and soda water to wine glass
full of ice.

Stir, garnish and serve.

strawberry fields

1 camomile tea bag

2 measures gin

1 measure strawberry purée

2 teaspoons lemon juice

1 measure double cream

3 teaspoons egg white

3 measures soda water

1 strawberry, to decorate

Place the tea bag and gin in a cocktail shaker and leave to infuse for 2 minutes.

Remove the tea bag, add ice, the strawberry purée, lemon juice, double cream and egg white to the shaker.

Shake and strain into a wine glass and top with soda water.

Garnish and serve.

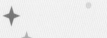

tijuana sling

1 ¾ measures tequila gold	Pour the tequila, crème de cassis, lime juice and bitters into a cocktail shaker.
¾ measure crème de cassis	
¾ measure fresh lime juice	Add some ice and shake vigorously for 10 seconds.
2 dashes of Péychaud bitters	
4 measures ginger ale	Pour into a highball glass then top with ginger ale.
	Garnish and serve.

To decorate
lime wheels
blueberries

long blush

1 measure vodka

2 teaspoons honey

1 measure
pomegranate juice

2 teaspoons lime juice

1 measure rosé wine

5 mint leaves

2 measures
soda water

Add the vodka, honey, pomegranate and lime juices, wine and mint leaves to a cocktail shaker and shake.

Strain into glass and add the soda water.

Top the glass with crushed ice, garnish and serve.

To decorate

mint sprig

pomegranate seeds

pink
mojito

6 mint leaves, plus a sprig to decorate

juice of ½ lime

2 teaspoons sugar syrup

3 raspberries

1 ½ measures white rum

½ measure Chambord liqueur

cranberry juice, to top

Muddle the mint, lime juice, sugar syrup and raspberries in a highball glass.

Add some crushed ice and pour in the rum and Chambord.

Stir well, add more ice, top with cranberry juice, garnish and serve.

spirit
forwards

bittersweet symphony

1 measure gin

1 measure Campari

½ measure passion
fruit syrup

½ measure fresh
lemon juice

lemon slices,
to decorate

Put the gin, Campari, passion
fruit syrup and lemon juice into
a cocktail shaker with some ice
and shake to mix.

Strain into an old-fashioned glass
over ice, garnish and serve.

cherry julep

juice of ½ lemon
1 teaspoon sugar syrup
1 teaspoon grenadine
1 measure cherry brandy
1 measure sloe gin
2 measures gin
lemon twists,
to decorate

Add ice, lemon juice, sugar syrup, grenadine, cherry brandy, sloe gin and gin into a cocktail shaker, and shake until a frost forms on the outside of the shaker.

Fill a highball glass with crushed ice.

Strain the cocktail into the ice-filled glass, garnish and serve.

spiced
berry julep

✦

1 tablespoon frozen mixed berries, plus extra to decorate

1 measure cinnamon and nutmeg-infused bourbon

6 mint leaves, plus an extra sprig, to decorate

2 teaspoons sugar syrup

Put the berries, bourbon and mint in a glass and muddle.

Leave to stand for 5 minutes, then add the sugar syrup and half-fill the glass with crushed ice and churn with the muddler.

When it is thoroughly mixed, top the glass with crushed ice.

Garnish and serve.

silk stocking

drinking chocolate powder	Moisten the rim of a chilled cocktail glass and dip it into the drinking chocolate powder.
¾ measure tequila	
¾ measure white crème de cacao	Pour the tequila, white crème de cacao, cream and grenadine into a cocktail shaker filled with ice.
4 measures single cream	
2 teaspoons grenadine	Shake for 10 seconds and strain into the chilled glass.

autumn
dawn

½ measure vodka
½ measure Cointreau
1 teaspoon fresh
lemon juice
1 teaspoon Chambord
liqueur

Put the vodka, Cointreau and lemon juice into a shaker with some ice and shake briefly.

Strain into a shot glass and carefully drop in the Chambord.

valentine martini

2 measures raspberry vodka

6 raspberries, plus extra to decorate

½ measure lime juice

1-2 dashes sugar syrup

To decorate
pomegranate seeds
dehydrated lemon

Add all the ingredients to a cocktail shaker filled with ice, and shake until a frost forms on the outside of the shaker.

Double-strain into a chilled martini glass.

Garnish and serve.

pink angel

½ measure
white rum

¼ measure Advocaat

¼ measure
cherry brandy

1 egg white

½ measure
double cream

Put ice into a cocktail shaker with the rum, Advocaat, cherry brandy, egg white and cream and shake well.

Strain into a chilled cocktail glass and serve.

pink lady

2 ½ measures Plymouth gin

1 measure Calvados or applejack brandy

1 measure fresh lemon juice

½ measure grenadine

1 fresh egg white

cocktail cherry, to decorate

Put the gin, Calvados, lemon juice, grenadine and egg white into a cocktail shaker with ice and shake vigorously.

Strain into a chilled cocktail glass and serve.

watermelon martini

1 ½ measures vodka

½ measure passion fruit liqueur

4 chunks watermelon

1 dash cranberry juice

watermelon wedge, to decorate

Put all of the ingredients in a cocktail shaker.

Add ice and shake.

Strain into a chilled martini glass, garnish and serve.

pink gin

3–4 dashes Angostura bitters	Shake the bitters into a glass filled with ice.
2 measures gin	Add the gin and stir.
lemon peel twist, to decorate	Strain into a chilled cocktail glass, garnish and serve.

bellini-tini

2 measures vodka

½ measure
peach purée

½ measure
peach schnapps

4 drops of
peach bitters

2 peach wedges,
to decorate

Put ice into a cocktail shaker,
add the vodka, peach purée,
peach schnapps and peach
bitters and shake vigorously.

Strain into a chilled cocktail
glass, garnish and serve.

sours

strawberry daiquiri

3 strawberries, hulled

dash of strawberry syrup

6 mint leaves, plus a sprig to decorate

2 measures golden rum

2 measures lime juice

strawberry slice, to decorate

Muddle the strawberries, syrup and mint leaves in the bottom of a cocktail shaker.

Add the rum and lime juice, shake with ice and fine-strain into a chilled martini glass.

Garnish and serve.

swallow dive

1 measure honey vodka	Put some ice into a cocktail shaker with all the other ingredients. Shake well.
1 measure Chambord	
1 measure lime juice	Strain in an old-fashioned glass over crushed ice.
4 raspberries, plus extra to decorate	Top with more crushed ice, garnish and serve.

pink clover club

juice of 1 lime

dash of grenadine

1 egg white

3 measures gin

strawberry slice,
to decorate

Put ice into a cocktail shaker.

Pour the lime juice, grenadine,
egg white and gin over the
ice and shake until a frost
forms, then strain into a chilled
cocktail glass.

Garnish and serve.

strawberry & mint daiquiri

3 strawberries

dash of strawberry syrup

6 mint leaves

2 measures golden rum

1 measure fresh lime juice

To decorate

strawberry slice

mint sprig

Muddle the strawberries, syrup and mint leaves in the bottom of a cocktail shaker.

Add the rum and lime juice, shake with ice and fine-strain into a chilled cocktail glass.

Garnish and serve.

french pink lady

2 measures gin
4 raspberries
1 measure Triple Sec
3 teaspoons lime juice
1 teaspoon pastis
lime wedge,
to decorate

Add the gin, raspberries, Triple Sec, lime juice and pastis to a cocktail shaker and muddle.

Fill the shaker with ice and shake, then strain into a glass.

Garnish and serve.

vanilla daisy

2 measures
Bourbon whiskey

1 measure fresh lemon
juice

1 measure
vanilla syrup

1 teaspoon grenadine

2 cocktail cherries, to
decorate

Put the Bourbon, lemon juice
and vanilla syrup into a cocktail
shaker with some crushed ice
and shake vigorously.

Strain into an old-fashioned
glass filled with crushed ice
then drizzle the grenadine
through the drink.

Garnish and serve.

pink coconut daiquiri

2 measures white rum

1 measure coconut liqueur

2 measures fresh lime juice

1 teaspoon grenadine

lime slice, to decorate

Put the crushed ice into a cocktail shaker.

Pour the rum, coconut liqueur, lime juice and grenadine over the ice, and shake vigorously until a frost forms.

Strain into a cocktail glass, garnish and serve.

cosmopolitan

1½ measures lemon vodka	Add all the ingredients to a cocktail shaker.
4 teaspoons Triple Sec	Shake and strain into a glass.
3 teaspoons lime juice	Garnish and serve.
1 measure cranberry juice	
lemon peel, to decorate	

jack rose

2 measures
apple brandy

3 teaspoons grenadine

4 teaspoons
lemon juice

Add all the ingredients to a cocktail shaker.

Shake vigorously, then strain into a glass and serve.

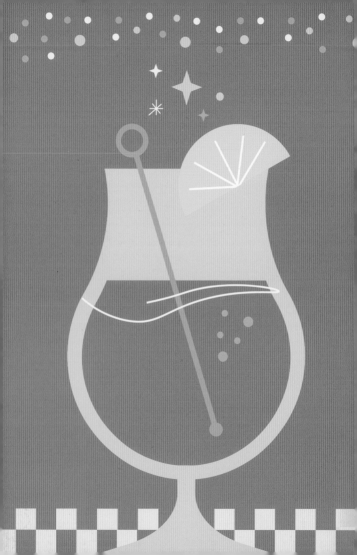

sharers
& punches

sex on the beach

makes 2-3

2 measures vodka

2 measures peach schnapps

2 measures cranberry juice

2 measures orange juice

2 measures pineapple juice

To decorate

cherry

mint sprig

Put ice into a cocktail shaker and add the vodka, schnapps and fruit juices.

Shake vigorously.

Put ice into highball glasses, strain over the cocktails.

Garnish and serve.

pink
sangria

3 measures rosé wine

2 teaspoons
agave syrup

2 measures
pomegranate juice

2 measures lemon
verbena tea

2 measures soda water

pink grapefruit slice,
to decorate

Pour the rosé wine into a glass,
add 1 teaspoon of the agave
syrup and stir until it dissolves.

Fill the glass up with ice and
add the remaining agave syrup,
the pomegranate juice, lemon
verbena tea and soda water.

Garnish and serve.

blush sangria

makes 1 large jug

Add all ingredients to a jug, then fill the jug with ice.

Stir, garnish and serve.

4 measures vodka

2 measures crème de framboise

200 ml (7 fl oz) rosé wine

6 measures cranberry juice

2 measures lime juice

1 measure sugar syrup

6 measures soda water

edible flower petals, to decorate

poppin's gin fizz

makes 4

4 measures gin

1 ½ teaspoons agave
syrup

250 ml (8 fl oz)
sparkling wine

250ml (8 fl oz)
hibiscus tea

4 measures pink
grapefruit juice

raspberries,
to decorate

Add the agave syrup and gin
to a large jug and stir until the
agave syrup dissolves.

Fill the jug with ice and add
the hibiscus tea, pink grapefruit
juice and wine and stir.

Garnish and serve.

tinto de vevezia

makes 1 large jug

4 measures Aperol

4 measures pink
grapefruit juice

4 measures
orange juice

200 ml (7 fl oz)
rosé wine

4 measures soda water

To decorate
orange slices
grapefruit slices

Fill a jug with ice.

Add all the ingredients to the jug and stir.

Garnish and serve.

torino spritzer

makes 1 large jug

4 measures sweet vermouth

4 measures Campari

4 measures Triple Sec

4 measures lemon juice

200 ml (7 fl oz) lemon soda

200 ml (7 fl oz) red wine

To decorate

lemon slices

orange slices

grapefruit slices

Fill a jug with ice.

Add all the ingredients to the jug and stir.

Garnish and serve.

la rochelle punch

makes 1 large jug

4 measures Cognac

50 g (2 oz) frozen
mixed berries, plus
extra to serve

4 measures
apple juice

2 measures
lemon juice

2 measures sugar syrup

300 ml (½ pint)
ginger ale

Add the Cognac and berries
to a food processor or blender
and blend until smooth.

Pour into a jug.

Add plenty of ice and the
remaining ingredients to the jug
and stir.

Garnish and serve.

sherry punch

5 pineapple chunks

5 raspberries, plus extra to decorate

3 lemon slices

2 measures fino sherry

2 teaspoons sugar syrup

To decorate
pineapple wedge
raspberry

Add the pineapple chunks, raspberries, lemon slices and sugar syrup to a cocktail shaker and muddle.

Add the sherry and shake.

Strain into a glass full of crushed ice, garnish and serve.

watermelon punch

makes 3-4

1 watermelon (around 9 kg/20 lb)

200 ml (7 fl oz) vodka

20 mint leaves

3 measures lemon juice

5 measures sugar syrup

lemon wheels, to decorate

Cut the top off the watermelon and use a spoon to scoop out the flesh inside. Set aside the hollowed-out watermelon.

Carefully remove the pips from the watermelon flesh, then add the flesh and all the remaining ingredients to a food processor or blender and blend until smooth.

Pour into the hollowed-out watermelon, garnish and serve with straws.

champagne & prosecco

bellini

½ ripe white peach	Put the peach, raspberry and sugar syrup into a food processor or blender and blend until smooth.
1 raspberry	
2 teaspoons sugar syrup	
5 measures Prosecco, chilled	Strain into a flute glass, top with the Prosecco and serve.

champino

1 measure Campari

1 ¼ measures sweet vermouth

Champagne, to top

lemon twist, to decorate

Pour the Campari and sweet vermouth into a cocktail shaker filled with ice.

Shake, then strain into a chilled cocktail glass.

Top with chilled Champagne, garnish and serve.

rossini

4 strawberries	Put the strawberries and sugar syrup into a food processor or blender and blend until smooth.
2 teaspoons sugar syrup	
5 measures Prosecco, chilled	Strain into a flute glass, top with the Prosecco and serve.

riviera fizz

1 ½ measures
sloe gin

½ measure fresh
lemon juice

½ measure
sugar syrup

Champagne, to top

lemon twist,
to decorate

Put the sloe gin, lemon juice
and sugar syrup in a cocktail
shaker filled with ice and shake.

Strain into a chilled flute, top
with Champagne and stir gently.

Garnish and serve.

parisian fizz

4 teaspoons
raspberry purée

2 teaspoons passion
fruit pulp

1 teaspoon sugar syrup

1 teaspoon pastis

4 measures
chilled Prosecco

raspberry, to decorate

Add all the ingredients to a flute
glass and stir.

Garnish and serve.

negroni sbagliato

1 measure Campari

1 measure
sweet vermouth

2 measures Prosecco

orange, to decorate

Add the ingredients to an old fashioned glass filled with ice and stir.

Garnish and serve.

To decorate

lemon twist

cocktail cherry

french 66

1 white sugar cube

6 dashes
orange bitters

1 measure sloe gin

juice of ¼ lemon

Champagne, to top

lemon twist,
to decorate

Soak the sugar in the bitters
then drop it into a flute glass.

Add the sloe gin and lemon
juice and stir.

Top with chilled Champagne,
garnish and serve.

blackwood blush

2 measures
grapefruit juice

2 measures rosé wine

2 teaspoons creme
de mûre

Prosecco, to top

To decorate

grapefruit slice

thyme sprig

Add all the ingredients except
the Prosecco to a wineglass
filled with ice.

Top with chilled Prosecco, stir
gently, garnish and serve.

cobbler fizz

3 slices mandarin

2 raspberries, plus extra to decorate

2 teaspoons sugar syrup

1 measure fino sherry

4 measures Prosecco

Add the mandarin, raspberries and sugar syrup to a cocktail shaker and muddle.

Add the sherry and shake.

Strain into a flute glass and top with chilled Prosecco.

Garnish and serve.

italian dandy

1 measure cognac

1 teaspoon
cherry brandy

1 teaspoon
sugar syrup

Prosecco, to top

lemon twist,
to decorate

Pour the cognac, cherry brandy
and sugar syrup into a cocktail
shaker or mixing glass filled
with ice.

Stir for 10 seconds and strain
into a flute.

Top with chilled Prosecco,
garnish and serve.

head
over heels

juice of 1 lime

1 teaspoon sugar syrup

2 measures vodka

3 drops Angostura
bitters

pink Champagne,
to top

1 strawberry,
to decorate

Pour the lime juice, sugar syrup,
vodka and Angostura into a
cocktail shaker filled with ice
and shake until a frost forms.

Pour without straining into
a highball glass, top with
Champagne, garnish and serve.